LONELY PEOPLE

by Warren W. Wiersbe
Associate Bible Teacher
Back to the Bible Broadcast

A
BACK TO THE BIBLE
PUBLICATION

Back to the Bible
Lincoln, Nebraska 68501

65,000 printed to date—1983
(5-2350—65M—103)
ISBN 0-8474-6509-8

Printed in the United States of America

Contents

Chapter 1

The Meaning of Loneliness

> Alone, alone, all, all alone,
> Alone on a wide wide sea!
> And never a saint took pity on
> My soul in agony.

So wrote Samuel Taylor Coleridge in 1798 in his famous poem "The Rime of the Ancient Mariner," a poem you probably had to read when you were in high school. He also wrote in that poem:

> . . . This soul hath been
> Alone on a wide wide sea:
> So lonely 'twas, that God himself
> Scarce seemèd there to be.

Have you ever felt like that? Or have you ever tried to help somebody who felt like that? Loneliness isn't a new problem, is it? Loneliness has been with us for a long, long time.

The psalmist wrote in Psalm 102: "Hear my prayer, O Lord, and let my cry come unto thee. Hide not thy face from me in the day when I am in trouble; incline thine ear unto me; in the day when I call, answer me speedily. For my days are consumed like smoke, and my bones are burned like an hearth. My heart is smitten, and withered like grass, so that I forget to eat my bread. By reason of the voice of my groaning, my bones adhere to my skin. I am like a pelican of the wilderness; I am like an owl of the desert. I watch, and am like a sparrow alone upon the housetop" (vv. 1-7).

Perhaps you can identify with the psalmist in his loneliness. It seems strange in a world experiencing a population explosion that loneliness is one of man's greatest problems. Loneliness is something we must not overlook, because loneliness is serious.

Consequences of Loneliness

Loneliness has physical consequences. It's interesting to note that one survey reported that more than 50 percent of the heart patients admitted that they were lonely and depressed before they had their heart attack. Some research indicates that there's a relationship between loneliness and certain kinds of cancer. Loneliness has physical consequences.

Loneliness also has emotional consequences. I found in one study that 80 percent of the psychiatric patients who were interviewed said that they sought help because of their loneliness. Loneliness leads people to become nervous and start to overeat, to drink and to experience insomnia. Half a million people attempt suicide in the United States every year, and many of these attempts are linked to loneliness. People get lonely, and they feel like destroying themselves. At the Los Angeles, California, Suicide Prevention Center, many of the teen-

6

agers interviewed confessed that their attempts to take their lives started with feelings of loneliness.

Yes, loneliness has physical consequences and emotional consequences, and it also has spiritual consequences. You see, God made us, not to be lonely but to fellowship with Him and with His people. He made us that we might have lives that are creative, lives that are growing, lives that enjoy enrichment. It's a sad thing when people are lonely and fail to achieve all that God wants them to achieve in their lives.

As we consider the meaning of loneliness, let's try to answer three very important questions.

Definition of Loneliness

What is loneliness?

Like many other feelings in our lives, it's easier to experience it than it is to define it! Loneliness is being all by yourself even when you're surrounded by people. Loneliness is a feeling of isolation even in the midst of a crowd. You feel unwanted. You feel unneeded. You feel as though there's nothing to live for. You feel as though nobody really cares anymore. That's loneliness. Loneliness eats away at the inner person. It saps you of strength. It robs you of hope. Loneliness, as it were, puts a wall around you no matter how free you may be.

What It's Not

We should distinguish between loneliness and solitude. Solitude is simply physical isolation, and solitude is good for us. Our Lord Jesus used to go out by Himself to meditate and to pray. The Apostle Paul at one time left his friends that he might walk to a certain place while they traveled by ship. He wanted solitude. He wanted to be alone.

In my own life, I find that every day I must get off by myself just to think, to meditate and to pray. I need to have my inner man "ventilated," as it were. Solitude is good for us. The Word of God tells us that it's good to be alone with God, to be alone to face yourself and to meditate, to think and to pray.

We should note that loneliness is not the same as being lonesome. All of us have had the experience of being lonesome. In my own travels, when I've been away from my family, I've had that temporary feeling of being lonesome. But when you're lonesome, you know it's going to end. You're going to hop a plane and fly home. Or the meeting's going to end, and you'll drive home. Or your friends or loved ones who are away from home will return to you. Being lonesome is not as deep as being lonely. It doesn't hurt quite as much. Sometimes we have the feeling of being forlorn. Being forlorn is being lonesome plus experiencing grief and sadness. Often we're forlorn when we lose a loved one, and we know we won't see that person again until we get to heaven, provided that the loved one was born again through faith in Jesus Christ.

What It Is

No, loneliness is not the same as solitude, being lonesome or being forlorn. Loneliness is that inner feeling of being isolated and insulated, unwanted,

8

unneeded, uncared for; and lonely people are people who hurt.

I have pastored three churches, each of them in a metropolitan area, and I've noticed that the presence of many people is no protection against loneliness. In fact, crowds can make it worse. When lonely people walk the streets of the city or go into the restaurants or to the park and see other people having a good time and laughing, it makes their own pain that much greater.

People who feel lonely often think of destroying themselves at the holiday seasons—during the Thanksgiving season, the Christmas season, the spring season—when people who have families and loved ones are rejoicing. Lonely people feel terribly devastated during these holidays because they can't enter into the joy of others.

This is God's invitation: "Ho, every one that thirsteth, come to the waters, and he that hath no money; come, buy and eat; yea, come, buy wine and milk without money and without price" (Isa. 55:1). Now listen to this: "Why do ye spend money for that which is not bread? And your labor for that which satisfieth not? Hearken diligently unto me, and eat that which is good, and let your soul delight itself in fatness" (v. 2).

Let me give you my own definition of loneliness: Loneliness is the malnutrition of the soul that comes from living on substitutes. That's what Isaiah 55 is talking about. You're spending money for that which is not bread. You're laboring for that which doesn't satisfy. God offers you what is worthwhile, the things that satisfy, and He offers them "without money and without price" (v. 1). That's the unbounded, unlimited grace of God.

People today have the idea that if you have money, a job and food, you'll be satisfied. And yet, Isaiah was saying, in effect, "Well, you do spend your money, but you aren't buying bread. You are laboring, you do have a job, but it doesn't satisfy. Oh, you're eating, but it doesn't do you any good. You're living on substitutes!"

Loneliness is the malnutrition of the soul that comes from living on substitutes. And the sad thing is, many of the people I meet are *satisfied with substitutes*. They're satisfied with entertainment when God offers them joy. They're satisfied with taking a sleeping pill when God offers them peace. They're satisfied with prices when God offers them values. They're satisfied with fun when God offers them abundant life. They're satisfied playing a role in society when God wants to make them His own children.

Causes of Loneliness

What causes loneliness?

People have been studying loneliness for many years. Sociologists have examined the subject. So have psychologists and other medical experts.

Social Causes

Social causes contribute to loneliness. The mobility of modern life leaves many people rootless. Today we have many "casual contacts" but very

10

few friendships. How many of the people on your street do you know? How many of the people in your apartment do you know? How many of them do you *want* to know? Until the recent economic crunch, 20 percent of the American population relocated every year. This means digging up your roots and being transplanted! This means having to make new friends. But most people don't make new friends that quickly. What causes loneliness? Sometimes mobility will do it.

I think the *competitiveness* of life also helps to cause loneliness. We're all so busy succeeding! We're so busy taking care of number one! We're so busy focusing on ourselves that we forget about other people. The competition of life forces people *from* us instead of drawing people *to* us.

I think some people are lonely because of *fear*. Real dangers exist in our big cities as well as in our small towns. Elderly people are afraid of being attacked. Those who live in apartments have double and triple locks on their doors. They're afraid to speak to strangers, and perhaps you can't blame them.

You mix together the mobility of modern life, the competitiveness of life, fear and the fact that we live in a very *impersonal* society, and you can easily understand why some people are lonely. When you go to the bank, you aren't a name, you're a number. When you go into a store, you're a credit card. People don't know our faces, and they don't remember our names. Yes, there are social causes of loneliness.

Psychological Causes

Loneliness also has *psychological* causes. I've noticed in my own pastoral ministry that the people who are lonely often have similar characteristics. For one thing, they *hurt*. Somewhere in life they've been hurt. They've either been turned down by an employer or they have been rejected by a friend or by someone they thought they might want to marry, and they hurt inside. They are afraid of being hurt again. They carry unhealed inner wounds, and because these people hurt, they keep their distance. When they look at you, they say, "Well, you may hurt me; so I don't want to get too close to you."

Lonely people are not only hurting people, they are also sometimes *guilty* people. Often they are carrying around a dirty conscience, or they're regretting past mistakes and past sins.

They are often *insecure* people. It takes security to be able to reach out to others. You have to know where *you* stand and who *you* are and what *you* can do to be able to reach out to others, because others may be a threat to you. Insecurity never built strong relationships.

Lonely people are often *confused* people. They aren't sure who they are or where they're going or why they're here.

Sometimes lonely people are *selfish* people. They are governed by self-pity. They feel sorry for themselves. Others have more than they have. Others can do more than they can do. Instead of being thankful for what they *do* have, they sit around feeling sorry for themselves because of what they *don't* have! My Bible tells me, "A man who hath friends must show himself friendly" (Prov. 18:24).

Spiritual Cause

But I really believe that the root cause of loneliness is the *spiritual* cause. Spiritual relationships are the most important relationships of your life. Life is built on relationships—your relationship to yourself, to others and to God. Being able to know yourself, accept yourself and be yourself enables you to relate to others. I have learned that when my relationship to God, to myself and to others is what it ought to be, loneliness is not a problem.

Cure for Loneliness

Is there a cure for loneliness?

Yes, there is. Perhaps we can't change society too much, and we can't force others to change. Some lonely people may need professional Christian counsel. If your loneliness is bordering on depression and destruction, then you ought to get professional counseling from a Christian. But we can experience inner healing if we'll just trust Jesus Christ. He can restore broken relationships—with God, with ourselves and with others. Jesus Christ can help us to know ourselves, to accept ourselves and to be ourselves. Only Jesus Christ can cleanse us from our guilt of sin and give us a brand-new future. Only Jesus Christ can make us new people

13

and give us the inner power to face life and handle its demands.

Loneliness may have social causes, but basically loneliness is an "inside problem." It can be solved only in the heart. That's why Jesus says, "Behold, I stand at the door, and knock; if any man hear my voice, and open the door, I will come in to him, and will sup with him, and he with me" (Rev. 3:20). Jesus Christ wants to move into your life and get acquainted with you and have you get acquainted with Him. He wants to cleanse you and make you a new person. Then you and Jesus together can solve these problems that have been causing loneliness in your life.

Is there a cure for loneliness? Jesus Christ is the only One I know who can give you eternal life and abundant life. That's why He came and died, and that is His offer to you today.

Chapter 2

Cain: The Loneliness of Sin

We all know that Cain killed Abel, but did you know that Cain also killed Cain? Cain committed "spiritual suicide" and brought upon himself a life of wandering, aimlessness and loneliness.

Life consists of living relationships. If I may use an image, life is made up of open doors. Most important is the open door to God that comes through faith. When you put your faith in the Lord Jesus Christ, it opens a door to a marvelous life for you. There is an open door to other people—your brother, your family, your friends, those around you. There must be an open door to yourself—you must know yourself, accept yourself, live with yourself and use what God has given you for His glory. Finally, there must be an open door to the world around you, to life around you. You should be able to enjoy the beauties of nature and the blessings that God has put into this wonderful world.

The tragedy of Cain's life was that *he closed all the doors!* The story is found in Genesis 4. Cain and his brother Abel came to the altar. Each offered a sacrifice. The tragedy is that Cain offered the wrong

15

sacrifice with the wrong attitude. He did not bring a sacrifice of faith.

"The Lord said unto Cain, Why art thou angry? And why is thy countenance fallen? If thou doest well, shalt thou not be accepted? And if thou doest not well, sin lieth at the door" (vv. 6,7). God talked to Cain about the doors in his life. The Hebrew says, "Sin is crouching like an animal at the door." If Cain opened that door and yielded to that temptation, it would spring on him and destroy him. Sad to say, that's exactly what Cain did. Cain went out into the field and killed his brother.

"And the Lord said unto Cain, Where is Abel, thy brother? And he said, I know not: am I my brother's keeper? And he said, What hast thou done? The voice of thy brother's blood crieth unto me from the ground. And now art thou cursed from the earth, which hath opened her mouth to receive thy brother's blood from thy hand; when thou tillest the ground, it shall not henceforth yield unto thee its strength; a fugitive and a wanderer shalt thou be in the earth. And Cain said unto the Lord, My punishment is greater than I can bear" (vv. 8-13).

It's too bad he didn't say, "My sin is greater than I can bear!" It's too bad he didn't ask for forgiveness, but he didn't.

"Behold, thou hast driven me out this day from the face of the earth; and from thy face shall I be hidden; and I shall be a fugitive and a wanderer in the earth; and it shall come to pass, that any one that findeth me shall slay me" (v. 14).

"Cain went out from the presence of the Lord"

(v. 16). He dwelt in the land of Nod, which means "wandering," east of Eden. There Cain built a city. And when you read about this Cainite civilization in Genesis 4:16-24, you find it was a great deal like our civilization today.

The problem that Cain had, of course, was the problem of closing the doors. He was a lonely man. He was a fugitive and a wanderer, not a pilgrim and a stranger. Those of us who have trusted Christ as our Saviour are pilgrims and strangers in this world. This world is not our home; heaven is our home. But there's a vast difference between being a pilgrim and a stranger and being a fugitive and a wanderer. The pilgrim knows where he is going and how he's going to get there. The fugitive—the wanderer—is looking for some destination, some quiet haven, someplace where he can be satisfied. How sad it was that Cain rejected the grace of God!

Let's notice the doors that Cain closed in his life. Because he closed them he ended up a lonely man.

Cain's Unbelief

First of all, *he closed the door on God by his unbelief.* God's way is always the way of faith. God had taught Adam and Eve, and they had taught their sons, that God's way is the way of faith. "Faith cometh by hearing, and hearing by the word of God" (Rom. 10:17). God had taught Adam and Eve the meaning of blood sacrifice. When God clothed them after their disobedience, He killed some animals and used the skins to cover their nakedness.

Cain knew this, and Abel knew it. When Abel

17

came to the altar, he brought the firstborn of his flock. He brought the very best he had, and he brought it as an act of faith. Cain came with the produce of his field, and he came in unbelief. The Bible calls this "the way of Cain" in Jude 1:11. Cain was religious, but he was rejected. Cain was sincere, but he was rejected. Cain wanted his own way—the way of human effort, the way of human merit—not the way of faith. And Cain closed the door on God by his unbelief.

The only thing that opens the door to God is faith. "Behold, I stand at the door, and knock," said the Lord Jesus. "If any man hear my voice, and open the door, I will come in to him, and will sup with him, and he with me" (Rev. 3:20). He also said, "I am the door; by me if any man enter in, he shall be saved, and shall go in and out, and find pasture" (John 10:9). He was talking about salvation, freedom and satisfaction. If you enter in by faith in Christ, you will be saved. You will go in and out—that's freedom. You will find pasture—that's satisfaction. But Cain closed the door on God because of his unbelief.

Have you done that? Have you really trusted Jesus Christ as your Saviour? You say, "Well, there are so many things about God I don't understand." Welcome to the club! I have been a Christian for many years, and the longer I walk with God, the more mysterious some things become, but the more wonderful they become! It is such a blessed experience to walk with the Lord, to have the door of your heart opened to Him and to be in fellowship with God. That's the first step toward conquering loneliness—open the door to God, get right with Him and have your sins forgiven through faith in Jesus Christ.

Cain's Hatred

Cain closed the door on God by his unbelief. But he closed a second door, and this made his loneliness even worse: *He closed the door on his brother by his hatred.*

Consider I John 2:9-11: "He that saith he is in the light, and hateth his brother, is in darkness even until now. He that loveth his brother abideth in the light, and there is no occasion of stumbling in him. But he that hateth his brother is in darkness, and walketh in darkness, and knoweth not where he goeth, because darkness hath blinded his eyes." You can understand, then, how Cain became a fugitive and a wanderer—because he hated his brother. Hatred creates darkness in the soul.

"In this the children of God are manifest, and the children of the devil: whosoever doeth not righteousness is not of God, neither he that loveth not his brother. For this is the message that ye heard from the beginning, that we should love one another. Not as Cain, who was of that wicked one, and killed his brother. And why killed he him? Because his own works were evil, and his brother's righteous" (3:10-12).

The Word of God makes it very clear that hatred closes the door on people. If in your heart there is hatred toward a brother, if you are holding a grudge

19

against somebody, it is no wonder you feel lonely. Don't make the same mistake that Cain made. Cain closed the door on God through unbelief, and he closed the door on his brother through hatred.

You dare not separate these two. According to the great commandment (Matt. 22:34-40), we are to love God and also to love our neighbor. You can't say, "Well, my heart is open to God and I love God, but I hate my brother." The Word of God makes it very clear that love for God results in love for my brother. If I claim to love God, whom I cannot see, how can I hate my brother, whom I can see? (see I John 4:20).

Notice the stages in Cain's decision to close the door on his brother. First, he envied his brother. God showed respect to Abel and to his offering, but He did not show respect to Cain and to his offering. Cain was envious because his brother was accepted. That envy began to grow into anger and hatred. Jesus said that hatred in the heart is the moral equivalent of murder (see Matt. 5:22).

The next step was hypocrisy. Cain lied about his attitude. He went out into the field to talk to his brother, but Cain was really hiding his true intentions. Then he murdered his brother, and that closed the door.

Love always keeps the doors open. When you have a right relationship to God by faith, it will result in love for your brother. That means you will forgive your brother and be kind to him. "Be ye kind one to another, tenderhearted, forgiving one another, even as God, for Christ's sake, hath forgiven you" (Eph. 4:32).

Cain's Dishonesty

Cain closed the door on God because of his unbelief, and he closed the door on his brother by his hatred. Then *he closed the door on himself by his dishonesty.*

You have to live with yourself. Wherever you go, you are there. In Genesis 4:9, God said to Cain, "Where is Abel, thy brother? And he said, I know not." Cain was a liar. "Am I my brother's keeper?" The answer is yes! We are to love our neighbor—our brother—even as we love the Lord. Cain lied to God, and he lied to himself. He was a child of the Devil.

In I John 3:12 we are told that Cain was "of that wicked one." John 8:44 informs us that Satan is a liar and a murderer. This is why Cain was "of that wicked one." He was a liar and a murderer. He lied to God, and He lied to himself. He was a murderer—he killed his brother. He closed the door on himself by his dishonesty.

There is a great need today for integrity. Integrity means wholeness of the inner person. Integrity means being honest with oneself. Shakespeare said in *Hamlet,* "To thine own self be true." Integrity is an important part of life, especially of the Christian life. The Lord Jesus said we shouldn't be double-minded and we shouldn't have a double outlook on life. "If, therefore, thine eye be healthy [single], thy whole body shall be full of light" (Matt. 6:22). But if your outlook is double—if you are looking at God with one eye and at the world with the other—then you will not have integrity. Your life will be characterized by duplicity and hypocrisy.

Cain closed the door on himself by his dishonesty. I wonder if you are being dishonest with yourself? Perhaps you blame other people for what's happened to you. Maybe you blame God for what's happened to you. Have you ever thought of blaming yourself? Have you ever thought of looking into the mirror and saying, "Here is the problem"? Cain closed the door on himself by his dishonesty.

Repentance involves honesty. When a person repents, he is being honest with himself and honest with God. He is saying, "I am the culprit! I am the one who is to blame!" Are you blaming your brother or your sister for that family problem? Are you blaming the boss or your fellow workers for that difficulty in the office or in the shop? If you look in the mirror, you will find out who the real culprit may be.

Cain's Despair and Loneliness

Finally, *Cain closed the door on life itself by his despair and his loneliness.* He said, "My punishment is greater than I can bear" (Gen. 4:13). Why didn't he confess his sin? Why didn't he trust the grace of God? He simply wouldn't do that. "Behold, thou hast driven me out this day from the face of the earth" (v. 14).

22

If you're not in a right relationship with the Creator, you won't be in a right relationship with any of the creation. We sing in one of our songs, "This is my Father's world." When you know God as your Father, then His world becomes a place where you can enjoy Him and serve Him. But if you don't know Him, if you've closed the door on Him, then this world becomes a prison. It becomes a concentration camp. No matter where you turn, there is no satisfaction. You have closed the door on life itself by your despair.

"I'm a wanderer!" cried Cain. "I'm a fugitive!" What did Cain do to try to solve his problem? Cain tried desperately to conquer his loneliness *by building a city*. Cain had been a farmer. Then he built a city. Cain had been a tiller of the soil. Then he introduced the manufacturing of various tools and weapons from bronze and iron. Cain started a civilization.

Our present civilization is the consequence of what Cain did. We're back to human effort again. Cain was saying, "We can work and be satisfied. We can build culture. We shall have tents and cattle, yes, but we shall also have music, and we shall have things made of iron and bronze. We shall have craftsmen make artistic things for us." Culture is a fine thing if it glorifies God, but it is a tragic substitute if God is left out.

We find in Cain's civilization the breakdown of the home. Lamech had two wives. God's standards for marriage were rejected. Cain tried to build culture without God. He tried to get a crowd around

23

him to have activity, to distract him from the loneliness of sin. What happened? Did it solve the problem? No!

I think it was Thoreau who said that a city is a place where hundreds of people are lonely together. I have pastored in the city. I have walked the streets of the city, and I have seen the lonely faces there. It all started with Cain. He built himself a hell on earth, but he thought it was a heaven on earth. His city had things and activities but no satisfaction, no salvation. He lived in the midst of a prison, and he thought he was having a great time.

The loneliness of sin. Sin is at the root of much loneliness. I'm not saying that everybody who is lonely is like Cain—an awful sinner. Sometimes loneliness stems from other experiences. But many people need to admit they have closed the door on God by their unbelief. They have closed the door on their brother by their hatred. They have closed the door on themselves by their dishonesty. And as a consequence, they have closed the door on the world and on life around them because of their despair and lack of sincere repentance. They are living on substitutes.

May I remind you of my definition of loneliness? Loneliness is the malnutrition of the soul that results from living on substitutes.

Cain had a great civilization! In his city were many people with much opportunity and all kinds of culture and activity, science and development, even technology; but Cain was still a fugitive and a wanderer on the earth.

24

The loneliness of sin.

The Lord Jesus Christ invites you to come and receive salvation: "I am come that they might have life," He said, "and that they might have it more abundantly" (John 10:10). Open your heart to Him!

Chapter 3

Job: The Loneliness of Suffering

Except for our Lord Jesus Christ, probably no person named in Scripture suffered as much as did Job. The Book of Job describes his situation to us. Job lost his wealth in one day. He lost all of his children in one day. And then he lost his health. He lost the love of his wife. He lost the compassion of his friends. But he never really lost his faith in God. In the Book of Job we are introduced to a man who knew how to suffer.

Job said about his life, "I loathe it; I would not live always. Let me alone; for my days are vanity" (Job 7:16). Literally, he was saying, "My days have no meaning."

He later said, "Are not my days few? Cease then, and let me alone, that I may take comfort a little" (10:20).

Job knew the loneliness of suffering. Suffering often results in loneliness, doesn't it? When we are suffering, we are prone to lose our perspective on life. Little things become big, and big things become much smaller. We focus on ourselves, not on others. When you hurt, you are especially conscious of your own mind and body. When you hurt, you start questioning your faith, you start worrying, you become afraid. So often suffering results in loneliness.

Description of Job's Suffering

Let's look at several aspects of Job's experience. Perhaps we can discover in the Word of God the encouragement we need when we are suffering and when we feel lonely.

An Animal in a Net

Job 19 gives Job's interpretation of his situation. It's a very interesting chapter, filled with pictures— vivid pictures—of what he was going through. Verse 6 says, "Know now that God hath overthrown me, and hath compassed me with his net." This is the first picture he gave as he described his suffering: He saw himself as an animal caught in a net. "God hath overthrown me, and hath compassed me with his net."

In the previous chapter, Job's friend Bildad talked about Job's situation, and he warned Job, "He is cast into a net by his own feet, and he walketh upon a snare. The trap shall take him by the heel" (18:8,9). Bildad said, in effect, "You're going to trap yourself, Job." But Job said, "No, God is the One who has trapped me in the net."

When you suffer, you feel as if you are trapped. You feel confined. All of a sudden you have lost your liberty. All of a sudden you are in a cast or wearing a brace or in a hospital bed. All of a sudden

27

the doctor says you cannot work. You are suffering, and you feel trapped—like an animal in the net.

A Criminal in Court

A second picture of Job's suffering is found in Job 19:7: "Behold, I cry out of wrong, but I am not heard; I cry aloud, but there is no justice." One translation says, "Behold, I cry out because of violence" (Berkeley). Job pictured himself as a criminal in court. He was standing before God, the Judge, and he was saying, "This is wrong! Why should this happen to me? I cry aloud, but there is no justice." He felt guilty. He felt that God was unfair. He cried out, but God didn't even answer. That's a part of the loneliness of suffering. We cry out to God, and sometimes God doesn't answer right away. The silence of God makes our loneliness hurt that much more. Our faith is on trial. We stand in court, but there is nobody, apparently, to defend us.

Sometimes suffering does that to us. Suffering brings back old guilt, the memory of past sins, the regrets of past errors and mistakes. We have a lot of time on our hands while we lie in a hospital bed, and we feel like a criminal in court.

A Traveler at a Roadblock

In Job 19:8 we see a third picture: "He [God] hath fenced up my way that I cannot pass, and he hath set darkness in my paths." Job felt like a traveler at a roadblock. He was saying, "Here I was, making such good progress, going forward. I was raising my children, and I was enjoying my life. I was serving

28

God." (And he was. We must never get the idea that Job had been living a wicked life. Job had been living a life of service to glorify God.) "Now," he said, "I'm like a traveler who can't go any farther. There's a roadblock in front of me. If I turn to the right, there's a hedge. If I turn to the left, there's a ditch. I can't go backward. I can't go forward."

Have you ever felt that way when you've been suffering? All of your plans are changed, and you have to stand still. There were so many things you were going to do, and then you had a heart attack. There were so many plans you were going to fulfill for yourself and your family, and then there was an auto accident. You became a traveler at a road-block, unable to make progress. It's no wonder Job was frustrated. He was like an animal in a net, a criminal in a courtroom, a traveler at a roadblock.

A Dethroned King

In Job 19:9 we read: "He hath stripped me of my glory, and taken the crown from my head." Job saw himself as a king who had been dethroned. He lost his glory.

He certainly had lost his *physical* glory. Job was sitting on the ash heap, covered with sores. He was ugly. When people looked at him, they shook their heads, closed their eyes and turned away.

He had lost his *financial* glory. He was bankrupt. He had lost every bit of his financial resources. People were laughing at him behind his back. They were poking fun at him now that he was poor.

29

There was a time when Job was "on the throne." He told people what to do. He was respected; he was obeyed. But now, there he was on an ash heap, a broken man with a broken body, a man with no future. He was like a king dethroned.

How many times in my pastoral ministry I have visited executives in hospitals—men who were accustomed to signing checks for thousands of dollars, men who were used to giving orders to scores of people. And yet there they were in that hospital bed, with some anonymous nurse's aid telling them what to do! They were like a king dethroned.

A Building Being Destroyed

Job 19:10 says, "He hath destroyed me on every side, and I am gone." It is the picture of the destruction of a building. Our body is like a temple, a building. When you are suffering, you feel as if that building is being torn down, that God and His "demolition crew" have attacked you. There is pain, and sometimes the building doesn't function as it should! When suffering comes, it is so hard just to be normal, just to function the way we want to function! Job saw himself as a building being destroyed.

An Uprooted Tree

And then he saw himself as an uprooted tree: "And mine hope hath he removed like a tree" (Job 19:10). The Hebrew word "removed" is the word "uprooted." Job said, "Here I was with my roots

30

down deep, and I was growing and bearing fruit. There were people who found shade under my branches. Now I am cut down!" Job was a beautiful tree, and then along came the storm and uprooted the tree. It looked as though Job had no future.

If you pull up a tree by the roots, the tree will die. When you lose the roots in your life, there is not much future left. Your hope is gone.

An Enemy Beseiged by God

Finally, Job saw himself as an enemy beseiged by God's army: "He hath also kindled his wrath against me, and he counteth me unto him as one of his enemies. His troops come together, and raise up their way against me, and encamp round about my tent" (Job 19:11,12). Job felt like an enemy beseiged by God. He experienced fear and danger. It seemed as if God were against him. He could say with Jacob, "All these things are against me" (Gen. 42:36).

Results of Job's Suffering

We can well understand why Job would feel lonely. Having described his suffering, Job then showed the results of this suffering (Job 19:13-21). "He hath put my brethren far from me, and mine acquaintances are verily estranged from me" (v. 13). That's loneliness. "My kinsfolk have failed, and my familiar friends have forgotten me" (v. 14). Has that ever happened to you? "They that dwell in mine house, and my maids, count me as a stranger;

31

I am an alien in their sight. I called my servant, and he gave me no answer; I entreated him with my mouth" (vv. 15,16).

You would think that a servant, who is being paid by the master, would respond; but the servant would have nothing to do with Job!

"My breath is strange to my wife, though I make supplication to the children of my own body" (v. 17). ("I am loathesome to my own brothers" is another translation (NASB). Job's children had been killed in the storm; so he was talking about his relatives.) He said, "My wife thinks my breath is offensive. My own relatives will not have anything to do with me."

"Yea, young children despised me" (v. 18). Often young children are very sympathetic toward people who are older and who are hurting. "Yea, young children despised me; I arose, and they spoke against me. All my inward friends [my confidants, the people who are close to me] abhorred me, and they whom I loved are turned against me."

No wonder he cried out in verse 21, "Have pity upon me, have pity upon me, O ye my friends; for the hand of God hath touched me." He felt alienated from everyone. This is the cry of loneliness! Job was once great in stature, in wealth, in power and authority and in godliness, but now he was rejected and forgotten, even by his closest friends.

This is the loneliness that comes when we are suffering. It doesn't have to be physical affliction, it can be emotional affliction. It can be a broken heart as well as a broken body. Job was talking about the loneliness of suffering.

32

Cure for Job's Suffering

What is the answer to this? I don't want to give only the diagnosis of the case. When you are suffering and when you feel lonely and when people have forgotten you, what is the answer? The answer is found in Job 19:25,26. The answer is Jesus Christ. "For I know that my redeemer liveth, and that he shall stand at the latter day upon the earth; and though after my skin worms destroy this body, yet in my flesh shall I see God."

What was Job testifying about here? He was saying, "I have a living Redeemer!" Job didn't know as much about Jesus Christ as we do; therefore, our faith ought to be greater than his was. Job said, "I have a living Redeemer who one day is going to stand on this earth and make everything right. It's not important that I have everything my way today. What is important is that one day God will have everything His way when the Redeemer comes."

When you have a living Saviour, *then you have a living hope!* "In my flesh shall I see God" (v. 26). Job was referring to resurrection. The doctrine of the resurrection is found in the Old Testament. It is not taught as clearly as it is in the New Testament, but it is there. Job was looking forward to that time when all of his suffering would be over, all of his trials would end, and instead of suffering he would enjoy glory.

When you realize that Jesus Christ is your Saviour, that Jesus Christ is the Redeemer, that one day Jesus Christ will return and make everything the way it's supposed to be, it gives you hope. Even though your friends may forsake you, even though your family may neglect you, even though the servants and the children may not pay any attention to you, *Jesus is always there.*

Christ Sets Us Free

Let's go back to the pictures that Job gave of his suffering and see what a difference Jesus can make. Job felt like an animal confined in a net. And yet with Jesus Christ as your Saviour, you have freedom. "If the Son, therefore, shall make you free, ye shall be free indeed" (John 8:36).

In Philippians 4:11 Paul said, "I have learned, in whatever state I am, in this to be content." Paul was in prison. Like Job, he was like an animal in a net. And yet Paul said, "I am free! They might confine my body, but they can't confine my soul. I'm free in the Lord Jesus Christ!"

Christ Represents Us

Job felt like a criminal standing in court with no one to defend him. But Romans 8:38,39 tells us that nothing shall separate us from the love of Christ. Who can condemn us when Christ has died for us and today represents us in heaven before the throne of God? (v. 34). "There is, therefore, now no condemnation to them who are in Christ Jesus" (v. 1).

Christ Guides Us

Job felt like a traveler who was facing a roadblock. He didn't know which way to go. We know that Jesus Christ guides us. He is the Good Shepherd. "The steps of a good man are ordered by the Lord" (Ps. 37:23)—and so are the stops of a good man! Sometimes "he maketh me to lie down" (23:2). You may be in a situation now where God is making you lie down.

We Reign Through Christ

Job felt like a king who had been dethroned, but as Christians we are not dethroned. Romans 5:17 tells us that we "reign in life by one, Jesus Christ."

We Are Built Up Eternally in Christ

Job felt like a building being torn down. But we read in II Corinthians 4:16: "For which cause we faint not; but though our outward man perish, yet the inward man is renewed day by day." We do not look at the things that are seen; we look at the things that are *not* seen. Why? Because the things that are seen are temporal—they aren't going to last—but the things that are not seen are eternal. We know that we have a "house not made with hands, eternal in the heavens" (5:1).

We Are Rooted in Christ

Job felt like a tree being uprooted; he had lost his hope. But as Christians, we are rooted in Jesus Christ. We have a living hope because we belong to the living Saviour, the Lord Jesus Christ. We have been born again "unto a living hope" (I Pet. 1:3).

35

Job felt as if God were his enemy. But God is not our enemy. God is our Friend and God is our Father. We are "reconciled to God by the death of his Son" (Rom. 5:10). We are reconciled to God!

What I'm saying is this: Don't go by your feelings, go by the Word of God. If you go by your feelings, you will feel just the way Job felt. You will feel as if you are trapped in a net, as if you are condemned in a court, as if you are standing at a roadblock, unable to make any progress. You will feel like a king who's been dethroned, like a building that is being destroyed, like an uprooted tree or like an enemy being beseiged. When Jesus Christ is your Saviour, when He moves in and controls, He makes the difference between defeat and victory. When Jesus Christ is standing with you, when He's praying for you, when He is strengthening you and enabling you to do what He wants you to do, then you don't go by your feelings. You go by faith in God's Word. You rest completely on the Word of God.

Are you feeling lonely today because of suffering? My word to you is simply this: Jesus Christ is there with you if you've trusted Him as your Saviour. If you know Him as your Lord, you can be encouraged today. "The sufferings of this present time are not worthy to be compared with the glory which shall be revealed in us" (8:18). Job said, "I know that my Redeemer lives. I can trust Him, and He will see me through!"

Chapter 4

Moses: The Loneliness of Service

"I am now the most miserable man living," wrote a famous American leader. "If what I feel were equally distributed to the whole human family, there would not be one cheerful face on earth. To remain as I am is impossible. I must die or be better."

Abraham Lincoln wrote those words during the dark days of the Civil War. Those words remind us of the loneliness of service, the loneliness of leadership. Have you ever considered that those who are in places of leadership can be very lonely at times?

What is there about leadership that creates loneliness? First of all, the position itself. Here's a person who's been put into a position of leadership. This means he must be *over* other people, heading other people. When Peter wrote to the elders in I Peter 5, he reminded them that they were *over* the people and yet they were also *among* the people. That's a very difficult position! Your pastor is one of the sheep, and yet he is the shepherd. The position of leadership creates loneliness.

I think, too, that those who are in places of leadership face the loneliness of making decisions. Harry S. Truman, when he was president of the

United States, said this: "To be President of the United States is to be lonely, very lonely, at times of great decisions." Having to make decisions creates loneliness because of the consequences that are involved. You make a decision, you sign a paper, you issue an order, and many people are involved in the consequences.

I think, too, that leaders are lonely because of the great demands on their time and their energy. Woodrow Wilson, when he was president of the United States, said this: "It's an awful thing to be President of the United States. It means giving up nearly everything that one holds dear. The presidency becomes a barrier between a man and his wife, between a man and his children."

I'm sure this is true in other areas of leadership as well. Sometimes it can be true even in the ministry. You may be in a place of Christian service. Perhaps the demands on your time have robbed you of precious time with your family. You are experiencing the loneliness of leadership, the loneliness of service.

I think one of the most lonely things about service is this: Those who are in leadership positions have to see farther and see deeper than most other people. God gives to leaders the vision of what can be done or the vision of what may happen. Sometimes the followers don't have that same vision. How many times Moses, Joshua, even our Lord Jesus Christ, were misunderstood because others did not catch the vision.

And, of course, people who are in places of leadership are the targets of criticism, of envy, of blame. They become scapegoats. Service is not easy. It may be a great privilege. It certainly is wonderful to be called of God to serve, whether you are a Sunday school teacher, chairman of a committee, chairman of a board in a church, pastor, missionary, executive. But no matter where you serve, you will discover the loneliness of service.

Moses discovered this. He went through a very difficult experience when he was leading the Jewish people in the wilderness. The experience is recorded in Numbers 11. "And the mixed multitude that was among them fell to lusting, and the children of Israel also wept again, and said, Who shall give us flesh to eat? We remember the fish which we did eat in Egypt freely; the cucumbers, and the melons, and the leeks, and the onions, and the garlic. But now our soul is dried away: there is nothing at all, besides this manna, before our eyes" (vv. 4-6). For a year they had been eating the manna that came down from heaven every morning, except on the Sabbath Day, and now they were tired of it.

Numbers 11:10-15 says, "Then Moses heard the people weep throughout their families, every man in the door of his tent; and the anger of the Lord was kindled greatly. Moses also was displeased. And Moses said unto the Lord, Wherefore hast thou afflicted thy servant? And wherefore have I not found favor in thy sight, that thou layest the burden of all this people upon me? Have I conceived all this people? Have I begotten them, that thou shouldest say unto me, Carry them in thy bosom, as a nursing

39

father beareth the nursing child, unto the land which thou didst swear to give unto their fathers? From where should I have flesh to give unto all this people? For they weep unto me, saying, Give us flesh, that we may eat. I am not able to bear all this people alone, because it is too heavy for me. And if thou deal thus with me, kill me, I pray thee, out of hand, if I have found favor in thy sight, and let me not see my wretchedness."

Before you criticize Moses for expressing himself this way, you had better walk in his shoes for a while! He had all the Children of Israel to take care of. They were a brand-new nation and were just learning what it meant to walk with God and to follow a leader. They were a nation of slaves, liberated from Egypt, and Moses was trying to mold them into a great nation.

Leadership is not easy; leadership is difficult. Service is not easy; it is demanding. When you are discouraged and lonely in your service for Christ and you feel like giving up, just remind yourself of some of the lessons that Moses learned when he felt like giving up.

People Are Always People

Lesson number one: *Remind yourself that people are always people.* People are prone to complain simply because complaining is human. So often I've had the privilege of sharing in the installation service for a pastor at a church. Often it's a young pastor, perhaps recently graduated from school, and he's about to enter into his ministry. At some point in my private conversation I try to say to this young man, "Now, just remember, these are *people* that you are pastoring. They aren't perfect. They never will be perfect until they see the Lord Jesus Christ."

People are always people. If you want to, you can avoid the problems of people just by avoiding people! *Don't* be a leader. *Don't* be in a place of service. Just go off in a corner someplace and live with yourself. But if you are going to be a leader, you must remember that people are always people. They are prone to complain. Instead of remembering the blessings and appreciating your ministry, they are going to think about all the things they don't have.

When I read Numbers 11:5, I'm shocked. "We remember the fish which we did eat in Egypt freely." Can you imagine that? *Freely!* It cost them something to have the fish and the leeks and the onions and the garlic. *They were slaves in Egypt!* They forgot all of that. They forgot all that Moses had done for them. They forgot all that God had provided for them and how He had guided them. People are always people. They are prone to complain.

Because people are always people they will think the past is always better. I don't know how many times I've heard that in my ministry. "Oh, when Pastor _____ was pastor of this church, those were the good old days." I once asked an older man what people were talking about in the good old days, and he said, "Well, they were talking about the good old days." People forget the blessings of

41

the present. People are not excited about the prospects of the future. They want to live in the past. The past is always better.

Because people are always people, they tend to exaggerate their problems. Everything that comes along is the worst thing that ever happened.

Because people are always people, they have a tendency to lose their spiritual momentum. When Israel was delivered from Egypt, they were at a great peak spiritually. They were delivered in great power. They went through the Red Sea. They sang a song of victory. Then they began to complain. God met the need. They started complaining all over again, and God had to discipline them.

People have a tendency to lose their spiritual momentum. The monotony of the land was bothering them. The monotony of the diet was bothering them. They were getting accustomed to their blessings.

I notice something else—people are always influenced by others. The mixed multitude was that unbelieving Egyptian crowd. They were not Jewish people. They were Egyptians who had traveled during the exodus and left Egypt with the Jewish nation. The mixed multitude—this unconverted crowd—likes to complain. In every church and every Sunday school class are people who like to complain. The tragedy is that complaining and discouragement always spread, and they spread rapidly.

This is the first lesson you should remember when you are discouraged, lonely and tempted to give up: *People are always people.* Have high ideals for God's people, but be a realist. People are always people.

Everything Looks Worse Than It Is

A second lesson is this: *The situation always looks worse than it really is.* The Israelites were crying out for something to eat, and Moses was saying to God, "Where can I get flesh to feed all of these people?" I notice in Numbers 11:11-14 that Moses repeated the phrase, "All this people." The situation always looks worse than it really is, especially when you walk by sight and not by faith.

When Israel was delivered from Egypt, they stood at the Red Sea with the Egyptian army behind them, the desert around them and the sea before them. What could be more difficult? And yet God opened the way and saw them through. Later, they cried out for water, and God gave them water. They had to have food, so God gave them manna. One day the Amalekites showed up and declared war on them, and God gave Israel the victory. How prone we are to forget what God has done for us!

Charles Spurgeon used to say that we write our blessings in sand, and we engrave our complaints in marble. We forget what God has done.

If you are in a situation right now that looks very difficult, the Devil wants it to look far worse than it really is. Unbelief says, "Oh, it's terrible!" When the 12 Jewish spies went into the land of Canaan to survey the situation, they saw the giants and the high walls, but they didn't see God. They came back

43

and said, "We are like grasshoppers next to those great giants!" (see 13:33). They forgot God. God is not like a grasshopper. God is great! The situation always looks worse than it is if you get your eyes off God.

Leaders Often Magnify Their Own Importance

There is a third lesson: *It's very easy for leaders to magnify their own importance.* Moses started to pout. "Why have You afflicted Your servant? Why have I not found favor in Your sight. You've burdened me with all these people!" (see Num. 11:11).

I want to give Moses credit for expressing himself honestly. Moses didn't get up and make some pious speech. He went off and prayed and told God how he felt. That's a good way to pray.

When you read the Book of Psalms, you discover the psalmist didn't use artificial, pious prayers. He told God just how he felt. "My God, my God, why hast thou forsaken me? Why art thou so far from helping me?" (Ps. 22:1). But Moses was magnifying his own importance. *He* had to get food for all of the people. Nobody could do it but Moses!

Let me say a word to Sunday school teachers, pastors and missionaries. You and I are not responsible for the spiritual maturity or immaturity of our people if we have been faithful in feeding them. You couldn't have found a more faithful leader than Moses. In fact, the Book of Hebrews says he was faithful in all of God's house (Heb. 3:2,5). Moses was faithful to do what God gave him to do, and yet the people were still immature. Moses should not have

44

blamed himself, but he did magnify his own importance.

Don't have a "messianic complex." Don't think you have to solve every problem, perform every miracle or meet every need. God is the One who is in control. It is easy to magnify your own importance. Notice how many personal pronouns are in Moses' prayer! Moses was looking at himself instead of at God.

Leadership Is a Privilege

We need to learn a fourth lesson concerning the loneliness of service: *Leadership is a privilege, not a burden.*

Don't misunderstand me. There are burdens to leadership. I've pastored three churches. I've been a minister in two different parachurch organizations. I've done my share of ministering to missionaries. I realize that leadership can have its burdens. That's a part of life. You are a leader because God says, "I'll help you carry the burden. Somebody has to do this."

There are burdens in leadership, but Moses forgot about the *privileges*. "You have laid the burden of all these people on me. Have I conceived all these people? Should I carry them the way a father carries a little child?" (see Num. 11:11,12). They were like little babies; I would agree with that picture. "I am not able to bear all this people alone, because it is too heavy for me" (v. 14). Of course, that's true. God never expected him to carry all the burdens himself.

45

Moses lost the glow of leadership. Moses lost the excitement of the privilege of being God's chosen leader to serve Him. Perhaps your Sunday school class is breaking your heart just now, but it's a privilege to be teaching the Word of God. Maybe those people on that mission field are not responding the way they should. But it's a privilege to be sharing the Gospel with them! Your church is not growing as it should—that's true—but what a privilege to be one of God's servants! Remember, the angels in heaven would gladly exchange places with us. They would wait on the brink of glory and rush to have the privilege of preaching and teaching the Word of God. But God does not use angels. God uses weak vessels of clay like Moses—and like you and me.

God Will Solve the Problems

Leadership is a privilege, not a burden. There are burdens to leadership, but those burdens turn out to be blessings when we let God have control. And that's our final lesson. People are always people. The situation always looks worse than it really is. It is easy to magnify our own importance. Leadership is a privilege, not a burden. And finally, *God can and will solve all of the problems.* Just do what Moses did. Go to God in prayer. Tell Him how you feel. Tell Him what's wrong. Tell Him what you think needs to be done. And then listen to Him.

In the rest of Numbers 11, God told Moses what to do. God shared the blessing and shared the burden with 70 men of the elders of the people of

Israel. Talk to God. Listen to God. Trust God. Obey God.

Moses said, "I am not" (v. 14), but God's name is I Am. Whenever you say, "I am not," just remember God says, "I Am" (Ex. 3:14). God "is able to do exceedingly abundantly above all that we ask or think" (Eph. 3:20) because His calling is also His enabling. If God has called you, He will equip you. If God has called you, He will enlighten you. If God has called you, He will enable you. If God has called you, He will encourage you. He will see you through. Therefore, don't pray as Moses did, "Kill me. Take me away from my wretchedness" (see Num. 11:15). Instead, say, "Lord, You do the work, You get the glory. Give me what I need. Give me the divine enablement to glorify Your name," and God will see you through.

Yes, there is loneliness in service. There is also blessing in service as we seek to glorify the Lord Jesus Christ and patiently serve His people.

Chapter 5

Elijah: The Loneliness of Self-Pity

First Kings 19 introduces us to an event in the life of a great man—Elijah. The event is his loneliness and his discouragement.

I understand that more than four million people in the U.S. annually have to have special care because of depression. So often depression is a result of loneliness. Sometimes loneliness is a result of self-pity. We don't like to talk about self-pity because each of us likes to defend his own ego. But self-pity can be one of the most poisonous things in your system. When we start wallowing in self-pity and nurturing self-pity, we are opening ourselves up to all kinds of problems.

In I Kings 18 the great prophet Elijah had met and defeated the prophets of Baal. God had sent fire from heaven. God had answered prayer. The people had fallen on their faces, crying, "The Lord, he is God; the Lord, he is God" (v. 39). The prophets of Baal were slain by the servants of God. Then the rain came after three and one-half years of drought.

You would think that after all of this blessing

Elijah would have been walking on the mountain peaks of victory, that he would have been, as the young people say, "living on cloud 9." But just the opposite took place!

He was miserable!

"And Ahab told Jezebel all that Elijah had done, and how he had slain all the prophets with the sword. Then Jezebel sent a messenger unto Elijah, saying, So let the gods do to me, and more also, if I make not thy life as the life of one of them by tomorrow about this time. And when he [Elijah] saw that, he arose, and went for his life, and came to Beer-sheba, which belongeth to Judah, and left his servant there. But he himself went a day's journey into the wilderness, and came and sat down under a juniper tree. And he requested for himself that he might die, and said, It is enough! Now, O Lord, take away my life; for I am not better than my fathers. And as he lay and slept under a juniper tree, behold, an angel touched him, and said unto him, Arise and eat. And he looked, and, behold, there was a cake baked on the coals, and a cruse of water at his head. And he did eat and drink, and lay down again. And the angel of the Lord came again the second time, and touched him, and said, Arise and eat, because the journey is too great for thee. And he arose, and did eat and drink, and went in the strength of that food forty days and forty nights unto Horeb, the mount of God" (19:1-8).

Let's consider some of the truths that are found in this experience of Elijah's, truths that may help us in our own lives today.

Cost of Self-Pity

First of all, consider *the cost of self-pity.* Elijah was wallowing in self-pity. "I want to die!" he said. If he had really meant that, Jezebel would have taken care of it for him! Had Elijah really wanted to die, all he had to do was say to Jezebel, "Here I am, take my life." It was only self-pity.

Loss of Perspective

When we are encouraging self-pity, we lose our perspective. Everything becomes "out of joint." The little things become big, and the big things don't seem too important anymore.

Look at Elijah. He had just slain 850 false prophets, and yet one woman frightened him! Here was a man who had called down fire from heaven, and one woman frightened him. I know, she was the queen and she was vicious. But Elijah's self-pity caused him to lose his perspective. Just as Elijah did, we exaggerate the way we feel, and we exaggerate the circumstances around us. We exaggerate what other people are doing against us. We tend to lose our perspective when we are living in self-pity. Self-pity is an expensive luxury and a very terrible master.

Loss of Patience

Not only do we lose our perspective, but we also lose our patience. Elijah ran away from his place of duty. "When he saw that, he arose, and went for his life" (I Kings 19:3). He did not wait before the Lord and seek God's directions.

It is important to note in the life of Elijah that whenever he did something, it was because God told him to do it. "The word of the Lord came unto him, saying" is an oft-repeated phrase (17:2,8; 18:1). But this time we find Elijah impulsively, impatiently running ahead of God.

Be careful when you start getting nervous and fidgety, because you are liable to do some stupid thing. The Bible says, "He that believeth shall not make haste" (Isa. 28:16). Patience is important in the Christian life, but self-pity will lead you to impatience and disobedience.

Loss of Personal Touch

Self-pity is expensive. It not only causes us to lose our perspective and our patience, but it also causes us to lose our personal touch. We get isolated and insulated. Elijah, who should have been ministering to the people, ran off by himself. He even left his servant behind. There he was in solitude, and that solitude turned into loneliness.

We need others. We cannot make it by ourselves. The journey is too great for us. We must have the Lord, and we must have the Lord's people. I thank God for the Lord's people. They have been an encouragement to me and a help to me. At this point Elijah needed their help more than ever before. You say, "But he was a great prophet. He could pray, and marvelous things would happen." That is true. But he was also a man of like nature as we are, and he needed that personal touch.

51

Loss of Purpose

More than that, self-pity can cause us to lose our purpose. He said, "Let me die! Let me die!" God did not call Elijah to kill him. God called Elijah to use him to bring the people of Israel back to the worship of the true God.

I have often seen this in my ministry. Many times I get letters or phone calls from pastors who are having a rough time or from missionaries who are having a difficult time. They say, "You know, Brother Wiersbe, I'd just as soon throw it all overboard and quit! It's just not worth it!" They start praying as Elijah prayed, "Oh, let me die!"

Moses prayed this way in Numbers 11, didn't he? "If I'm going to be this wretched," said Moses, "then take my life" (see v. 15).

Consider the cost of self-pity. You and I can wallow in self-pity if we want to. God won't stop us. But what a terrible price we are going to pay!

Suppose God had answered Elijah's prayer. Suppose He had taken Elijah's life. What would this have meant to Elijah? God spoke to Elijah and told him to call Elisha as his successor. If Elijah had died, what would this have meant to the work of God? What would this have meant in the future of Israel? Elijah would have missed a glorious chariot ride to heaven if God had answered his selfish prayer!

If you find yourself wallowing in self-pity, enjoying it, licking your wounds, feeling sorry for yourself and blaming everybody else, just remember, you are paying a tremendous price.

Causes of Self-Pity

Consider next the *causes of self-pity.*

Physical

To begin with, there are often *physical* causes. James 5:17 tells us that Elijah was a man of like nature as we are. This man was tired. He was hungry. God said, "Elijah, take a good nap. Elijah, here is some food and some water." An angel came down and baked a cake for Elijah. Elijah was able to get strength from this nourishment that was provided for him.

Sometimes we who are in Christian service don't take care of our bodies as we should. We wonder why we are discouraged. We wonder why we are feeling sorry for ourselves. It could just be the chemistry of your body. It could just be that the most important thing you can do is to go to bed and take a nap. You say, "Some people do this too much." That may be so, but Elijah was tired, he was hungry, and his body was not functioning properly.

Emotional

More than that, there was an *emotional* cause to Elijah's self-pity. He had just been through a tremendous crisis on Mount Carmel with the strain of that all-day meeting. Pastors should be careful on Mondays because Mondays follow Sundays, and Sunday is the difficult day in their life. I know how many times on Monday morning everything seemed dark and dismal and discouraging. There are emotional causes for self-pity—when we go through

53

crisis experiences and when heavy demands are made on us.

Spiritual

There are also *spiritual* causes. I think that was the real problem for Elijah, although the other things entered in. To begin with, Elijah was guilty of unbelief. In I Kings 19:3 we read: "When he saw that, he arose." He was walking by sight and not by faith. He "went for his life" (v. 3). He was walking selfishly; he was not thinking about God's will.

Elijah felt that he had failed. He said, "I am not better than my fathers" (v. 4). Who said that he should be? His job was not to compete with the fathers! His job was to complete God's work. He felt he had failed, and that the people had failed. Don't compare yourself with somebody else.

When he met God at the cave, Elijah said, "I am the only one left" (see v. 10). God said, "There are seven thousand who have not bowed the knee to Baal" (see v. 18). Elijah felt that God had failed. He said, "God, why didn't You bring a great revival to the nation? Why aren't they worshiping You?" He was discouraged by a sense of failure.

Do you feel as if you've failed? Don't give up! Don't quit! Only God knows whether or not you have failed or succeeded. God rarely allows His servants to see all the good they are doing. One day in heaven you will find out what God has done through you. The important thing is not your self-esteem. The important thing is God's glory.

There are physical causes to self-pity. Maybe you

need a good night's rest, a good meal, some exercise, some ventilation. There are emotional causes. Maybe you have been through a tense, difficult time and need to relax. But fundamentally there are spiritual causes: unbelief, trying to keep up our own ego, forgetting about God's glory.

Cure for Self-Pity

What is the *cure for self-pity?*

Look to the Lord

To begin with, *look to the Lord.* In I Kings 19:8-18 we read that God met Elijah at Mount Horeb, and Elijah stood on the mountain. The wind went by, and the earthquake shook the mountain, and a fire came. But God was not in the wind or the earthquake or the fire. Then a still, small voice spoke to Elijah and told him what to do.

What is the cure for self-pity? First of all, *look to the Lord.* Just take yourself by the nape of the neck and shake yourself and say, "I'm not going to look at myself! I'm not going to look at the failures of the people! I'm not going to look at the circumstances. I'm going to look to the Lord." Elijah had not failed, the people had not failed, and the circumstances were just what God ordained them to be.

I like that little phrase the "still, small voice" (v. 12). God doesn't always accomplish His will in noisy ways. There is a *still* voice. God doesn't always use big things such as earthquakes and fire from heaven. There is the *small* voice. God's Word accomplishes God's will.

God has many tools. God can use the wind, the earthquake and the fire, but God prefers to use the Word, the still, small voice. So look to the Lord. Get your eyes off yourself.

Talk to the Lord

Second, *talk to the Lord*. Be honest with Him; tell Him how you feel. Tell Him that you hurt.

Listen to the Lord

Then, *listen to the Lord*. "Be still, and know that I am God" (Ps. 46:10). Listen to His Word. God will speak to you through His Word. God may speak to you through His people. Occasionally I've felt like Elijah, and I've gone to hear somebody preach, and the message I heard was just what my heart needed.

Wait on the Lord

Look to the Lord, talk to the Lord, listen to the Lord, and *wait on the Lord*. Wait for His time. Wait for His way. Wait, that you might be able to share in His glory.

Elijah learned that God had a plan. God said, "All right, I'm going to give you a successor—Elisha. I'm going to give you many victories. I'm going to accomplish many things through your life. And then I'm going to take you to heaven." The same God who begins the good work will complete it, because this is His promise in Philippians 1:6.

Let me warn you against self-pity. What is the cost of self-pity? You'll lose your perspective and your patience. You will impulsively do some foolish
56

thing. You will lose that personal touch and get isolated and lonely. You will lose the purpose God has for your life.

What are the causes of self-pity? Sometimes physical, sometimes emotional, always spiritual.

What is the cure? Look to the Lord, talk to the Lord, listen to the Lord, and wait on the Lord. "Wait on the Lord; be of good courage, and he shall strengthen thine heart" (Ps. 27:14).

Chapter 6

Mary and Martha:
The Loneliness of Sorrow

The most difficult kind of loneliness is the loneliness of sorrow, the loneliness that comes from bereavement. The Bible tells us that death is an enemy (see I Cor. 15:26). Yes, we know that we are going to go to heaven through faith in Jesus Christ. We know that our loved ones in Christ, when they die, go to be with the Lord. This comforts our hearts, but still our hearts hurt. Bereavement is something like an amputation: Part of you is cut off. People say, "Well, you had Mother or Dad for all these many years." That doesn't make it any easier, does it? In fact, it makes it harder.

It isn't wrong for Christians to sorrow. It's wrong for Christians to sorrow "as others who have no hope" (I Thess. 4:13). In the Word of God, you find God's people weeping when they go through the valley of the shadow of death.

Let's focus on John 11, the story of the resurrection of Lazarus. It's a familiar story. Lazarus was ill, and his two sisters sent a message to Jesus. "Lord, behold, he whom thou lovest is sick" (v. 3). Our

Lord tarried for two days, and during that time, Lazarus died. Then Jesus went to them, and by the time He got there, Lazarus had been in the grave for four days. But Jesus raised Lazarus from the dead! However, before He did that, He tenderly helped Martha and Mary as they shared their grief with Him.

Mary had been weeping in the house when Jesus arrived. Mary went out to see Jesus, and the neighbors who were there to comfort her said, "She goeth unto the grave to weep there" (v. 31). So Mary was weeping. And the friends were weeping. Verse 33 says, "When Jesus, therefore, saw her [Mary] weeping, and the Jews also weeping who came with her, he groaned in the spirit, and was troubled." And verse 35 says, "Jesus wept."

A great deal of weeping is recorded in this chapter, but Jesus did not criticize anyone for it. It isn't wrong for Christians to sorrow. It is wrong for Christians to sorrow as those who have no hope.

How can you find comfort and encouragement in times of loneliness and sorrow? You and I must claim the assurances that God gives us. John 11 contains a number of assurances that can help you in times of loneliness and sorrow.

God Loves You

First of all, you can be sure when you are going through times of sorrow *that God loves you.* I can understand why Mary and Martha might have questioned the love of the Lord Jesus. To begin with, their brother got sick. In verses 1, 2 and 3 of John 11 we are told that Lazarus was sick. Some people claim that if you are walking in the will of God, you won't be sick. But that wasn't true of Lazarus. We have no reason to believe that Lazarus was out of the will of God, and yet he became sick. The two sisters probably questioned the love of the Lord Jesus when they saw the disease in Lazarus.

Love and Suffering

Suffering is not incompatible with love. Some people say, "If God loved us, He'd keep us from having accidents, and He'd keep us from getting sick." Many times our sickness is our own fault, and our accidents come from our own carelessness. If God intervened every time we were heading for a calamity, this world would really be in a mess! No, suffering is not incompatible with love. The cross is proof of that.

Love and Delays

Mary and Martha might have questioned God's love because of our Lord's delay. "When he [Jesus] had heard, therefore, that he was sick, he abode two days still in the same place where he was" (John 11:6). The disciples might have argued, "If you really loved Lazarus, You would rush to Bethany now and heal his sickness." But Jesus didn't hurry. He waited. Love and delays go together.

Love and Disappointment

God's love could be questioned when we look at Lazarus' disease, our Lord's delay and also the sisters' disappointment. When Martha met the Lord Jesus, she said to Him, "Lord, if thou hadst been here, my brother had not died" (John 11:21). Mary said the same thing. "Lord, if thou hadst been here, my brother had not died" (v. 32). In verse 37, the Jewish friends who were visiting said, "Could not this man, who opened the eyes of the blind, have caused that even this man should not have died?"

So often when there is bereavement we say, "Oh, if we had only done this or that!" But such talk only makes the sorrow worse. God loves you. Circumstances and feelings may cause us to question that, but God loves us.

Love and God's Word

How do we know that God loves us? Because the Word of God tells us so. How did Mary and Martha know that Jesus loved them? The Word of God said so. "Now Jesus loved Martha, and her sister, and Lazarus" (John 11:5). The Word of God states very clearly that God loved these people. In spite of this love, there was sickness. In spite of this love, there was sorrow! *Never judge the love of God by your feelings or by your circumstances*. In fact, even the neighbors noticed the love that Jesus had because they said, "Behold how he loved him!" (v. 36).

How do we know that God loves us? Because God's Word tells us so. I read in Romans 8:35,37-39: "What shall separate us from the love of Christ? Shall tribulation, or distress, or persecution, or famine, or nakedness, or peril, or sword? . . . Nay, in all these things we are more than conquerors through

61

him that loved us. For I am persuaded that neither death, nor life, nor angels, nor principalities, nor powers, nor things present, nor things to come, nor height, nor depth, nor any other creation, shall be able to separate us from the love of God, which is in Christ Jesus, our Lord."

We know that God loves us because His Word tells us so. We know that God loves us because the Holy Spirit in our hearts tells us so. "The love of God is shed abroad in our hearts by the Holy Spirit who is given unto us," says Romans 5:5.

The greatest proof of God's love is the cross. "God commendeth [proves] his love toward us in that, while we were yet sinners, Christ died for us" (v. 8). Claim that first assurance when you feel the loneliness of sorrow; realize that God loves you.

Christ Is With You

The second assurance is *Christ is with you*. We today have an advantage that Mary and Martha did not have. Jesus had to *come* to Bethany. When He was here on earth, He was limited by His physical body. But our Lord Jesus Christ is *always with us!* "I will never leave thee, nor forsake thee" (Heb. 13:5).

He Knows Your Sorrow

Jesus Christ knows your sorrow. "Thou numberest my wanderings; put thou my tears into thy bottle. Are they not in thy book?" (Ps. 56:8). The suggestion here is that God keeps a record of your tears.

God knows your sorrow. You say, "But God is too busy running the universe to take care of my broken heart." Then read Psalm 147:3,4: "He healeth the broken in heart, and bindeth up their wounds. He appointeth the number of the stars; he calleth them all by their names." God is not so busy numbering and naming the stars that He doesn't see your broken heart or is unable to bind it up. The God of the galaxies is the God who heals the broken heart.

He Shares Your Sorrow

Christ knows your sorrow. *He shares your sorrow.* "Jesus wept" (John 11:35). The Lord Jesus is "a man of sorrows, and acquainted with grief" (Isa. 53:3). He groaned inwardly. He was indignant at the consequences of death and sin in this world.

He Can Transform Your Sorrow

He knows your sorrow, He shares your sorrow, and *He can transform your sorrow.* He said to Martha, "I am the resurrection, and the life; he that believeth in me, though he were dead, yet shall he live. And whosoever liveth and believeth in me shall never die" (John 11:25,26). When you have Jesus Christ as your Saviour, you don't have to worry about death. He transforms your sorrow, He sanctifies your sorrow, because He conquered death.

The Lord Jesus is "the resurrection, and the life" (v. 25). Death for the believer is only sleep. Jesus said in verse 11, "Our friend Lazarus sleepeth." In death, the believer goes to sleep. The body sleeps in the grave, the spirit goes home to be with the Lord.

Assurance number one is that God loves you. Assurance number two is that Christ is with you. He is "Emmanuel," or God with us (see Matt. 1:23).

God's Will Is Best

The third assurance is *God's will is best*. God has His times, and God has His purposes. The disciples couldn't understand why Jesus waited for two days. Jesus explained, "Are there not twelve hours in the day?" (John 11:9). In other words, "I'm on a divine timetable. I have My schedule. Don't rush Me." God has His times.

God also has His purposes. One purpose God was accomplishing was strengthening the people involved. Jesus said, "And I am glad for your sakes that I was not there, to the intent ye may believe" (v. 15). The faith of the disciples was increased by this experience.

The faith of Martha was also strengthened, and so was the faith of the Jews who came to see Mary and Martha. In fact, we are told that many of them believed in the Lord Jesus because of the raising of Lazarus (v. 45).

I don't know God's purposes in what you are going through. We all go through experiences and wonder why they are happening. Martha said, "Lord, if You had been here!" (see v. 21). Mary said, "Lord, if You had been here!" (see v. 32). The Jews said, "Oh, if He had been here!" Bury the alternatives. Forget about the "ifs." Just keep in mind that *God's will is best.* He has His times, and He will work out His purposes.

God Will Be Glorified If You Believe

A fourth assurance can comfort you when you are experiencing the loneliness of sorrow: *God will be glorified if you believe.* That's the promise that Jesus gave in John 11:4: "This sickness is not unto death, but for the glory of God, that the Son of God might be glorified by it." It's not important that you and I are pampered; it's not important that you and I have our own way. It is important that God is glorified.

You may say, "But that's a difficult experience for people to go through just for the glory of God." *But the glory of God is the most important thing in the universe!* It was difficult for Jesus to die on the cross for the glory of God, but He did it—and He did it for you. God will be glorified if you believe.

Jesus said to the people, "Roll the stone away!" (see v. 39). Martha said, "Please don't do that. He's been dead for four days, and by now he smells" (see v. 39). But Jesus said to her, "Said I not unto thee that, if thou wouldest believe, thou shouldest see the glory of God?" (v. 40).

The glory of God is the important thing. It's not important that you and I are comfortable. It is important that God is glorified. When our Lord thought about His own suffering and death, He said, "The hour is come, that the Son of man should be glorified" (John 12:23). Not crucified, but *glorified*.

Is that your prayer—that God shall be glorified? I know there are times when we hurt. There are times when we cannot be comforted. There are times when we feel so alone, especially during holiday seasons. We miss people who have been taken home to be with the Lord. But remember, one of these days God will be glorified if you believe.

He will be glorified in your life. You will grow in grace and in the knowledge of the Lord Jesus Christ.

He will be glorified through your testimony. "Then many of the Jews who came to Mary, and had seen the things which Jesus did, believed on him" (11:45). It's worth it all when people come to know Jesus as their Saviour.

"What shall it profit a man, if he shall gain the whole world, and lose his own soul?" (Mark 8:36). What shall it profit a Christian if he shall have his own way and souls are lost because of his selfishness?

God loves you. That's the first assurance you should claim. Christ is with you. You are not alone. God's will is best. You don't have to understand it, and you don't have to explain it. We don't live by explanations, we live by promises. God's will is best, and God will be glorified if you believe.

Jesus said to Martha, "Believest thou this?" (John 11:26). And she said to him, "Yea, Lord; I believe that thou art the Christ, the Son of God, who should come into the world" (v. 27). If you believe in Jesus Christ, then death has no terror for you. If you believe in Jesus Christ, then you can have the comfort of God today. The loneliness of sorrow is conquered by the presence and power of the Lord Jesus Christ.

Chapter 7

The Elder Brother:
The Loneliness of Stubbornness

Everybody was joyful and having a wonderful time. The fatted calf had been killed and roasted, and the whole village was celebrating the homecoming of a wayward boy. Everybody was joyful except for one man—the older brother. He was standing outside the house, angry, and he refused to go in. He was stubborn, and because he was stubborn, he was lonely. He might have called it "conviction," but really it was just plain, old-fashioned stubbornness! He was angry because he was not getting his own way.

Think with me about the loneliness of stubbornness. Let's examine our own hearts in the light of Luke 15:25-32: "Now his elder son was in the field; and as he came and drew near to the house, he heard music and dancing. And he called one of the servants, and asked what these things meant. And he said unto him, Thy brother is come; and thy father hath killed the fatted calf, because he hath received him safe and sound. And he was angry, and would not go in; therefore came his father out, and entreated him. And he, answering, said to his father, Lo, these many years do I serve thee, neither transgressed I at any time thy commandment; and yet thou never gavest me a kid, that I might make merry with my friends. But as soon as this, thy son, was come, who hath devoured thy living with harlots, thou hast killed for him the fatted calf. And he said unto him, Son, thou art ever with me, and all that I have is thine. It was fitting that we should make merry, and be glad; for this, thy brother, was dead, and is alive again; and was lost, and is found."

Our Lord gave the parable of the Prodigal Son in order to describe two kinds of sinners—fleshly sinners and self-righteous sinners. The Prodigal Son is a picture of people who are guilty of the sins of the flesh. He wasted his substance in riotous living. But the elder brother is a picture of those who are guilty of sins of the spirit. Everybody could see the sins of the Prodigal Son, but they couldn't see the sins of the elder brother. His sins were hidden in his heart until he opened his mouth and began to talk. The Prodigal Son was repentant and brokenhearted, but the elder brother was stubborn and proud, and he was a lonely man.

The Prodigal Son pictures the tax collectors and other sinners who gathered around the Lord Jesus to hear Him speak. The elder brother is a picture of the Pharisees and the scribes, who were very good at criticizing others but not quite so good when it came to judging their own hearts.

Many things were wrong with this elder brother, but one defect was obvious—he was a very stub-

born man. He was angry, and he would not go in.
There he stood, alone and lonely. Some families
have people like this as a part of their family tree.
These people won't come to any family gatherings
because they are carrying a grudge, they are angry
at somebody for something that happened years
ago. (Perhaps it might have been at the reading of a
will.) They will not come to the family gatherings;
they will not talk to some of their relatives. Of all
problems, family problems are the worst, and the
Devil likes to use them to create heartache and
sorrow.

Ungrateful to Your Father

Let's consider the sad consequences of stubbornness. To begin with, notice how this son was
treating his father. He was ungrateful to his father.
Stubbornness has a way of making us ungrateful
because we insist on having our own way. Instead of
being grateful for what we really do have, we're
ungrateful because of what we don't have. "Lo,
these many years I have worked for you, and you
never even gave me a little goat. But let this boy
come home, who has been wasting all of your
money in riotous living, and for him you kill not a
goat, but the best that we have—the fatted calf"
(see Luke 15:29,30). Families in that day kept a
fatted calf ready for a special occasion.

Notice how he mistreated his father. I note in
Luke 15:29 that the elder brother didn't even
address his father politely. In the East, when you
speak to your parents, you address them. You say
70

"Father" or you say "Mother." But this son started out and said, "Lo, these many years do I serve thee." He was not even polite to his father. He forced the father to come outside and talk to him. He wouldn't go in and talk to his father. That would have embarrassed the father.

He doubted his father's generosity. "All these years I've worked for you, and you've never given me anything!" (see v. 29). And yet his father was a very generous man.

He treated his father like an employer. "I've been working for you all these years!" Why hadn't he told his father that he wanted to have a party? He should have admitted to his father that he was lonely and wanted to have some of his friends come over. I'm sure the father would have let him do it—*if* the boy had any friends!

When we are stubborn, it shows that we are ungrateful to our Father. I think one of the best antidotes to loneliness is thankfulness—just being thankful to God. Over and over in the Word of God we are commanded to be thankful. When we pray, we should be thankful. "Make a joyful noise unto the Lord, all ye lands. Serve the Lord with gladness; come before his presence with singing. . . . Be thankful unto him, and bless his name" (Ps. 100: 1,2,4).

I wonder if we are ungrateful to our Father in heaven. All that He has is ours. That's an amazing thing! We are "heirs of God, and joint heirs with Christ" (Rom. 8:17). You may be complaining today because of something you don't have or because of

71

something that didn't happen. Just stop to thank God for all He has given to you and all He has done for you. Don't be ungrateful to your Father.

Unhappy With Your Work

Notice the consequences the elder brother suffered. How was he treating himself? He was unhappy. This son looked like a model worker. He was obedient. He never argued with his father. He was loyal. He worked hard in the field. It's possible for me to be laboring in the field, doing the Father's work, and still not be close to the Father's heart. He seemed like a model worker, but his heart was all wrong because he was a "drudge." He was doing his job because he *had* to do his job! Secretly, he was hoping to get something special, perhaps a big feast.

Many people carry with them a "hidden agenda." They do their work and take care of their family, but deep inside they have a hidden agenda. Sometimes you read in the newspaper about a well-known person who suddenly took off, left his wife and children (or her husband and children) and disappeared to start a new life. Why? Because for years they've been carrying this "hidden agenda" inside. They might be working in an office, but they really want to go to some exotic place and paint pictures. Or they've been driving a truck, but what they really want to do is fly a plane. The elder brother had a hidden agenda, and he finally admitted it.

Ephesians 6:6 tells us we should do the will of God "from the heart," not just because we have to! The Bible says, "Delight thyself also in the Lord, and he

shall give thee the desires of thine heart" (Ps. 37:4).
If I delight in the Lord, my desires will be the right
desires. And if my desire is to delight in the Lord and
please Him, then He will give me what I delight in.
But if my desires are selfish, then the Father, of
course, is not going to answer.

There was no joy in his labor, no enthusiasm. He
was not serving from the heart. He was stubborn.
Stubbornly he did his work, but he didn't do it
happily. He was ungrateful to his father. He was
unhappy in his own life.

Unforgiving Toward Your Brother

Notice his relationship to his brother: He was
unforgiving toward his brother. He did not love his
younger brother. After all, the younger brother
took his share of the inheritance and went off to a
far country, where he wasted it. He lost everything;
he ended up friendless, homeless, hungry and
homesick. Finally he said, "I'm going home" (see
Luke 15:18).

Did you ever notice what convinced the younger
son that he ought to go home? *It was the generosity
of his father.* "How many of my father's hired servants have bread enough and to spare, and I perish
with hunger!" (v. 17). It's the goodness of God that
leads us to repentance (see Rom. 2:4).

You would think that the elder brother would
have been watching for his brother to come home,
but he wasn't. He didn't love his brother. He was in
the field working when his brother came home. The
father welcomed his younger son and had the ser-

vants kill the fatted calf, and the party was already in progress *before the brother found out what was happening!* It's a sad thing when you don't even know what's happening in your own family. Sometimes people in your family can be ill or in the hospital, and you may not know about it. If we love one another, we keep in touch with one another.

The older son wasn't watching for his brother's return. Why? Because he didn't *want* him to come back! He was glad the boy was gone. As long as the younger son was gone, it made the elder son look good. But when the boy came home and said, "Father, I'm sorry, and I want to work for you," there was competition in the family.

He didn't even claim his brother. Did you notice that he said, "As soon as this, thy son, was come" (Luke 15:30). Not "this my brother" but "this thy son." Are there some of God's people you won't claim? Are you unloving toward your brother? He wouldn't even talk to him! He wouldn't go in and join the party. The father had to come out and talk to the elder brother. This is the tragedy of stubbornness.

Don't carry malice in your heart. Don't carry grudges. If you are going to have an enemy, get a good one, because an enemy is very expensive. He will give you headaches and backaches and ulcers and heart trouble, and he will hurt your fellowship with God.

The younger brother was a threat to him. As long as the boy was out in the far country sinning, it made the elder brother look good. As long as the younger brother was gone, the elder brother had more authority in the home. But the father loved his boy, and he was glad to have him come home. "Be ye kind one to another, tenderhearted, forgiving one another, even as God, for Christ's sake, hath forgiven you" (Eph. 4:32).

Is there someone in your family or in your church family whom you stubbornly refuse to talk to, whom you stubbornly refuse to make up with? "Well," you say, "I'm waiting for him to apologize." Perhaps so, but maybe you ought to go and say, "Look, let's talk this over."

The elder brother was building walls instead of bridges. He had built a wall between himself and his father, a wall between himself and his work, a wall between himself and his brother. He was a man who was ungrateful and unhappy and unforgiving.

Unloving Toward Others

And finally, he was unloving. One of the sad consequences of stubbornness is that it keeps everything down inside. There you are, cast in cement, unable to reach out in love to those around you.

It's interesting that this elder brother had no problem talking to the servant! He could speak to a servant, but he wouldn't talk to his brother. In fact, he had a difficult time talking to his father. He was unloving.

He had not really experienced the forgiveness of God. You have to *experience* forgiveness before you can *share* forgiveness.

In Matthew 18 we read our Lord's parable about the king who audited his books and discovered that one of his servants owed him millions of dollars. So he called the servant in and said, "I'm going to sell you into slavery" (see v. 25). The man fell down and begged the king to give him time to pay the bill. The king had compassion on the man and forgave him that huge debt. You would think that the man would have gone out and praised the Lord and been kind to everybody. No. Instead, he went out and found a servant who owed him a few dollars, and he said, "You pay me, or I'm going to put you in jail!" (see vv. 28-30). The man said, "Look, give me time" (see v. 29). But he did put him in jail. When the king heard about it, he said, "This is wrong. I forgave you that great big debt. Couldn't you forgive your fellow servant the small debt that he owed you?" (see vv. 32,33). And the king put the man in prison. Jesus said, "This is what your Father will do to you if you don't forgive your brother from your heart" (see v. 35).

When you *experience* God's forgiveness, you have no problem *sharing* God's forgiveness. This is the message that our Lord was trying to get across to the Pharisees. The Pharisees were proud, self-righteous, moral, upstanding people. They were religious people. They tithed. They prayed. They were very careful about their religion. But they had not really experienced God's forgiveness in their hearts.

I've noticed that this elder brother lacked all of the fruit of the Spirit. The fruit of the Spirit is *love—*

he doesn't show any love to his brother or to his father. *Joy*—he had no joy in his life. He was a drudge. He went to work every day and slaved just because he had to. He had no *peace*. He was causing a family feud! *Long-suffering?* Oh, no! He had no patience with anybody. He lost his temper, he was angry. *Gentleness?* Anything but gentleness! He was being very hard on his father and very hard on his brother. *Goodness?* No, he lacked goodness. *Faith?* Why didn't he believe what his father said? Why didn't he act on his father's word? He was a man who was very unloving toward those around him.

What he really needed was salvation. That was the message that Jesus was trying to get across. The publicans and sinners *knew* that they were lost; they knew they had to trust Jesus. The Pharisees and scribes thought, "We don't need to be saved. We are righteous." Our Lord was saying to them, "Oh, you're just the opposite! You *desperately* need salvation!"

We have learned from the elder brother that stubbornness leads to loneliness. If you are going to harbor ill will in your heart, if you are going to harbor malice, if you are going to carry grudges, you will be a very lonely person. You will end up being ungrateful to your Father, unhappy with your work and unforgiving toward your brother, and you will certainly be unloving toward those around you. Stubbornness has a way of robbing you of the things that really count—your Father's fellowship, your brother's love, joy with others, growing in your character.

The loneliness of stubbornness is some of the worst loneliness you can experience.

The question I'm asking you today is simply this: Are you on the outside? Is everybody else enjoying the Father's fellowship while you are outside? Is everybody else enjoying fellowship with one another while you are lonely? Why are you on the outside? Is it because you are stubborn? Is it because you refuse to submit to God? My plea to you today is this: "Humble yourselves in the sight of the Lord, and he shall lift you up" (James 4:10).

Chapter 8

Jesus Christ: The Answer to Loneliness

In these studies we have met seven different people, and we have discovered six different kinds of loneliness. The loneliness of sin was seen in the life of Cain. In Job, we discovered the loneliness of suffering. Moses taught us about the loneliness of service. Elijah the prophet warned us against the loneliness of self-pity. Mary and Martha told us how to have comfort in the loneliness of sorrow. The elder brother warned us about the loneliness of stubbornness. The final and the complete answer to all loneliness is faith in Jesus Christ. He is the answer to loneliness in your life.

Loneliness has been defined in many different ways. My own definition is this: Loneliness is the malnutrition of the soul that results from living on substitutes. "Ho, every one that thirsteth, come to the waters, and he that hath no money; come, buy and eat; yea, come, buy wine and milk without money and without price. Why do ye spend money for that which is not bread? And your labor for that which satisfieth not? Hearken diligently unto me, and eat that which is good, and let your soul delight

79

itself in fatness. Incline your ear, and come unto me; hear, and your soul shall live." That's God's invitation found in Isaiah 55:1-3.

God is saying to us today, "Why are you living on substitutes when you can have true, lasting blessings through faith in Jesus Christ?"

Let's take each of these persons we have been thinking about, and let's ask ourselves this question: What message would the Lord Jesus Christ give to each of them? What message would the Lord Jesus Christ give to Cain or to Job or to the elder brother? These messages would certainly be messages that you and I need to hear.

Christ Can Forgive You

Let's begin with Cain—the loneliness of sin. I believe that the message the Lord Jesus Christ would give to Cain is found in John 14:6: "I am the way, the truth, and the life; no man cometh unto the Father, but by me." Jesus said, "I am the way." The tragedy is that Cain had his own way. Jude 1:11 talks about "the way of Cain." What is the way of Cain? It's the way of religion without faith. It's the way of self-righteousness without the sacrifice of blood. It's the way of doing the best you can with what you have but not trusting in the Lord Jesus Christ. Jesus would say to Cain, "I am the way." If you ever hope to approach God, you must come through the Lord Jesus Christ.

Someone may say, "That sounds very exclusive! Are not all religions the same?" No, they are not. "There is no other name under heaven given among men, whereby we must be saved" (Acts 4:12). Cain had his own way. Jesus said, "I am the way."

"I am . . . the truth," is what our Lord said. Cain, you will remember, was a liar. He lied to his brother. Although he worshiped with his brother, he had murder in his heart. Cain lied to God: "Am I my brother's keeper?" (Gen. 4:9). He lied to himself. Cain was a liar. Jesus said, "I am . . . the truth."

The reason many people are lonely is because they will not face the truth. Jesus said, "And ye shall know the truth, and the truth shall make you free" (John 8:32).

Cain was a murderer, but Jesus said, "I am . . . the life." Cain murdered his brother, but in reality he murdered himself. He committed "spiritual suicide" by lying to God and murdering his brother.

Only Jesus Christ can give us eternal life. If you want to have eternal life, it has to come through Jesus Christ. Cain was a child of the Devil. First John 3:12 informs us that he was "of that wicked one." John 8:44 reminds us that Satan is a *liar* and a *murderer*. Cain was a liar and a murderer, born of the Wicked One.

Cain tried to solve his problems by building a city and living on substitutes. He carried his guilt with him. Jesus would say to Cain, as He says to us today, "I can forgive your sin, I can take away your guilt, I can give you a new beginning. I am the way, the truth, and the life; no man cometh unto the Father, but by me." If you are experiencing the loneliness of sin, that is the message you need. Trust Jesus Christ today.

God—Not Satan—Is in Control

What message would the Lord Jesus give to Job, who suffered so greatly? I think He would say to Job what He said to Peter and the apostles in Luke 22:31,32: "And the Lord said, Simon, Simon, behold, Satan hath desired to have you, that he may sift you as wheat; but I have prayed for thee, that thy faith fail not. And when thou art converted, strengthen thy brethren."

Job did not know that Satan was talking to God about him. Job did not know what was going on behind the scenes. It was important that Job *not* understand what was going on. He had to learn to trust God without explanations.

These verses from Luke 22 tell us that *God is in control, not Satan*. The sovereignty of God is so great that He can allow Satan to do his worst, and yet God can bring out His best. These words remind us that our suffering is working *for* us and not *against* us.

Our Lord described suffering as the sifting of wheat. Why would a farmer sift wheat? To get rid of the chaff. Why does God permit Satan to attack us? Why does He allow us to go through suffering? To sift us, to take out of our lives those things that are cheap and useless and to put into our lives those things that are good and lasting.

Our Lord said to Peter, "I have prayed for thee." The Lord Jesus upholds us in the furnace of affliction. Yes, God is in control. Suffering works for us because Jesus Christ upholds us and is praying for us in heaven. The result of all this is that God ministers through us to other people. "When thou art converted, strengthen thy brethren."

God did turn Peter around. God did change Peter, and Peter did strengthen others. In fact, in I Peter one of the major themes is suffering and glory.

If you are suffering today, remember, God is in control, not Satan. Your suffering can work for you, because Jesus is in heaven praying for you. Through this suffering, you can effectively minister to others to the glory of God.

Christ Wants to Share Your Burden

What message would the Lord Jesus Christ give to Moses? You'll remember how distraught and frustrated Moses was (Num. 11). The burden was so heavy! The work that he had to do was so great! His people were so ungrateful. He even wanted to die.

I think the message that Jesus would give to Moses is found in Matthew 11:28-30: "Come unto me, all ye that labor and are heavy laden, and I will give you rest. Take my yoke upon you, and learn of me; for I am meek and lowly in heart: and ye shall find rest unto your souls. For my yoke is easy, and my burden is light."

Moses was frustrated and feeling the weight of all the burden because he thought he had to carry it himself. Pastor friend, missionary friend, mother, dad, Sunday school teacher, please learn this: *The Lord Jesus Christ wants to carry the burden with you.* You say, "I have so many things I have to do. I can't accomplish them all." Not without the Lord Jesus. He said, "Without me ye can do nothing" (John 15:5). The Lord is not offering us rest *from* life but rest *in* life. He is not saying, "I will take your yoke away from you. You will never carry any burdens or have any responsibilities." That, to me, would not be a very happy life. I want to be involved in service. I want to be busy serving God the best I can. Christ is not offering us rest *from* life but rest *in* life. He is saying to us that we can carry the burdens and still have peace in our hearts. He is not talking about escape, He's talking about enablement. He says, "Come to Me. Quit looking at yourself, and quit looking at the circumstances. Take My yoke. Don't accept every job everybody gives you. Don't feel as though you have to do everything. Take the yoke that I give you. Spend time every day learning about Me. Get next to My heart, and you will find rest for your souls."

The yoke that He gives us is tailor-made. He knows exactly how we feel, and He knows just what we can take. He says, "I am going to be yoked with you. *Together* we are going to teach that Sunday school class. *Together* we are going to raise those precious children. *Together* we are going to pastor that church or work in that mission field." We are yoked with the Lord Jesus. This means we can carry burdens and still have rest in our hearts.

Serve Christ Rather Than Self

What would the Lord Jesus say to Elijah, who was filled with self-pity and wanted to die? I think the words of John 12:23-28 apply to Elijah: "And Jesus answered them, saying, The hour is come, that the Son of man should be glorified. Verily, verily, I say unto you, Except a grain of wheat fall into the ground and die, it abideth alone; but if it die, it bringeth forth much fruit. He that loveth his life shall lose it; and he that hateth his life in this world shall keep it unto life eternal. If any man serve me, let him follow me; and where I am, there shall also my servant be: if any man serve me, him will my Father honor. Now is my soul troubled; and what shall I say? Father, save me from this hour. But for this cause came I unto this hour. Father, glorify thy name."

The contrasts that our Lord presented here are very striking. He said, "You are either going to love your life, or you're going to lose your life for My sake. If you love your own life and try to take care of only yourself, you will lose your life. But if you lose your life for My sake, you will save it." You are going to either serve yourself or serve God. You are either going to run away or you are going to follow Christ, even to the cross. You are either going to be alone or you are going to be fruitful. You are either going to pray, "Father, save me!" or you are going to pray, "Father, glorify Thy name!"

You may be serving the Lord today, and you may feel like quitting. Please don't wallow in self-pity!

85

Lose your life for Jesus' sake. Serve God, not your own feelings. Follow Christ, even if it means crucifixion. You don't want to be alone. The loneliness of self-pity is tragic. You want to be fruitful. Let God plant you, and you will bear fruit for His glory.

Many times I've wanted to pray, "Father, save me!" but He has said, "No, I want you to pray, 'Father, glorify Thy name.' "

Christ Has Conquered Death

What would our Lord Jesus Christ say to Mary and Martha as they were going through the loneliness of sorrow? Just exactly what He *did* say: "Jesus said unto her, I am the resurrection, and the life; he that believeth in me, though he were dead, yet shall he live. And whosoever liveth and believeth in me shall never die. Believest thou this?" (John 11:25,26).

This is an interesting statement. Our Lord is saying, "It is not enough just to believe in a doctrine. You must have a living relationship with a Person—Jesus Christ."

Martha believed in the doctrine of the resurrection: "Martha saith unto him, I know that he shall rise again in the resurrection at the last day" (v. 24). Jesus said to her, "Martha, we don't have to wait until the last day. Wherever I am, there you will have resurrection and life" (see vv. 25,26).

You and I, as we go through the loneliness of sorrow, have Jesus at our side. We have the assurance of resurrection power. We have His abundant life. Those who die in Christ go to be with Him, and one day He shall raise them. Those who are alive when He returns shall never die. He asks us, "Do you believe this?" You say, "Yes, I do believe." Then you can experience the loneliness of sorrow and not break down and not blame God, because Jesus Christ is the Resurrection and the Life.

It's not that we simply believe a doctrine. We must be vitally related to the Person who has conquered death, Jesus Christ.

Forgive As Christ Forgave

Finally, what would our Lord Jesus Christ say to the elder brother? I believe that what He had to say in Matthew 6 would apply to the elder brother: "And forgive us our debts, as we forgive our debtors" (v. 12). "For if ye forgive men their trespasses, your heavenly Father will also forgive you; but if ye forgive not men their trespasses, neither will your Father forgive your trespasses" (vv. 14,15).

The elder brother was lonely because he was stubborn. He would not forgive. Forgiveness is a bridge over which all of us must cross at one time or another. You say, "Well, I won't forgive my brother." But someday he may have to forgive you, and then what will you do?

Our Lord is not teaching that we are saved by forgiving our brother. We are saved through faith in Jesus Christ. But if we have experienced God's forgiveness, we will want to forgive others and heed Paul's admonition: "Be ye kind one to another, tenderhearted, forgiving one another, even as God, for Christ's sake, hath forgiven you" (Eph. 4:32).

These then are the messages that Jesus would give to these people. If you are lonely today because of sin, He can forgive you. If you are lonely because of suffering, He can give you grace and strength. If you are lonely in your service, take His yoke and receive His rest. If you are lonely because of self-pity, give your life to Him in submission. If you lose your life, you will save it. If you are in the loneliness of sorrow, Jesus will give you comfort. If you are in the loneliness of stubbornness, He will help you to forgive and love others.

Don't be lonely today. Let Jesus change your life.